Presented to

_____

by_____

on_____

What Is the Bible?

Kathleen Long Bostrom
Illustrated by Elena Kucharik

Tyndale House Publishers, Inc.
CAROL STREAM, ILLINOIS

Visit Tyndale's exciting Web site for kids at www.tyndale.com/kids

TYNDALE is a registered trademark of Tyndale House Publishers, Inc.
Tyndale Kids logo is a trademark of Tyndale House Publishers, Inc.

Little Blessings is a registered trademark of Tyndale House Publishers, Inc.
The Little Blessings characters are a trademark of Elena Kucharik.

What Is the Bible?

Designed by Jacqueline L. Nuñez
Edited by Stephanie Voiland

Library of Congress Cataloging-in-Publication Data

Bostrom, Kathleen Long.
  What is the Bible? / Kathleen Long Bostrom; illustrated by Elena Kucharik.
    p. cm. -- (Little blessings)
  Includes bibliographical references and index.
  ISBN 978-1-4143-2012-0 (hc : alk. paper) I. Bible--Juvenile literature. I. Kucharik, Elena. II. Title.
  BS539.B68 2009
  220--dc22

                                        2008047827

Printed in Singapore

15 14 13 12 11 10 09
 7 6 5 4 3 2 1

To Elena:
Your beautiful paintings bring my words to life.
I am grateful for our partnership and our friendship.
Blessings of all sizes to you!

Also with gratitude to
Jan Axford, Stephanie Voiland, and Katara Washington Patton.
Thank you for your encouragement and guidance every step of the way!
—K. B.

For my Heartlights, Max and Luke.
I love you to pieces!
—E. K.

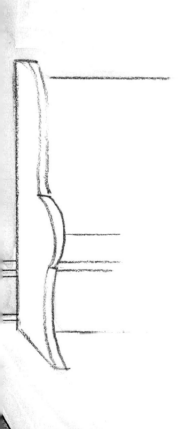

I've heard people talk

of the Bible in church.

It seems extra special,

so I'm on a search.

Who wrote the Bible?

One person? A few?

What does it say?

Can you give me a clue?

Is it a book

I will need as I grow?

Does it tell stories

of people I know?

What is the story

that God most enjoys?

Are there different Bibles

for girls and for boys?

Is it all true,

or is some just pretend?

Should I read it through

from beginning to end?

Does it have pictures

and puzzles and games?

How will I ever

remember the names?

If my Bible wears out,

should I throw it away?

Will God write another book

like it someday?

You're right that the Bible

is one of a kind.

There's no other book

that is like it, you'll find.

The Bible is more

than just any old book.

You want to know why?

Come with me! Take a look!

19

20

The Bible is special—

indeed, have you heard?

The Bible is also called

God's Holy Word.

It took many people

to write what's inside.

But God used the Spirit

to serve as their guide.

The Bible was not

written down at the start.

At first, people learned

all the stories by heart.

AMEN

amen

Though it was written

a long time ago,

the Bible's a book

you will never outgrow.

Inside the Bible,

there's much to explore—

with people you've heard of

and so many more.

Like Noah, who built

a gigantic, big boat,

and Joseph, so proud of

his colorful coat.

Esther, who wasn't

afraid of the truth,

and David's great-grandma,

a woman named Ruth.

That isn't all

that the Bible can hold.

It's where all the stories

of Jesus are told.

Learn of his birth on

the first Christmas Day.

Meet a few friends that

he made on his way.

He walked on the water

and calmed down the sea,

talked to the children

who sat by his knee.

Then comes the story

that God loves the best.

It's really no secret—

perhaps you have guessed!

It's the story of how

Jesus died on the cross.

It starts as a story

of sadness and loss.

41

But early on Easter,

folks saw with their eyes

that Jesus had risen—

oh, what a surprise!

God gave new life

to our Savior, his Son.

What an incredible

thing God has done!

You may see Bibles

in pink, blue, or green.

Some are so fancy,

they're fit for a queen!

It doesn't matter

what color you choose.

Inside, you'll find

God's amazing Good News.

The love that God has for us

shines through and through.

And that's how we know

that the Bible is true!

51

Some people read it all,
line after line.
Others may skip around—
both ways are fine.

What matters more

   is to read it and then

to go back and read it

   again and again!

You don't need puzzles

and games when you read.

Learning the stories

is all that you need.

God does not ask you

to know it all now.

Just try to live

as the Bible shows how.

59

If your Bible wears out,

it is really all right—

God thinks it's great

when you read it each night!

No other book will

replace it, no, never.

The Bible—God's Word—

will be with us forever!

Bible References

Here are some Bible verses to talk about as you read this book again with your child. You may want to open your Bible as you read the verses. This will help your little one understand that God's answers in this poem come from his Word, the Bible.

The Bible *is* special—indeed, have you heard?
The Bible is also called God's Holy Word.

> The word of God is alive and powerful. Hebrews 4:12

> The Word became human and made his home among us. John 1:14

It took many people to write what's inside.
But God used the Spirit to serve as their guide.

> All Scripture is inspired by God and is useful to teach us what is true. 2 Timothy 3:16

> When we tell you these things, we do not use words that come from human wisdom. Instead, we speak words given to us by the Spirit. 1 Corinthians 2:13

The Bible was not written down at the start.
At first, people learned all the stories by heart.

> I will teach you hidden lessons from our past—stories we have heard and known, stories our ancestors handed down to us. We will not hide these truths from our children; we will tell the next generation about the glorious deeds of the Lord. Psalm 78:2-4

Though it was written a long time ago,
the Bible's a book you will never outgrow.

> Your eternal word, O Lord, stands firm in heaven. Psalm 119:89

> You have been taught the holy Scriptures from childhood, and they have given you the wisdom to receive the salvation that comes by trusting in Christ Jesus. 2 Timothy 3:15

Inside the Bible, there's much to explore—
with people you've heard of and so many more.
Like Noah, who built a gigantic, big boat,

> When everything was ready, the Lord said to Noah, "Go into the boat with all your family." Genesis 7:1

and Joseph, so proud of his colorful coat.

> One day Jacob [Joseph's father] had a special gift made for Joseph—a beautiful robe. Genesis 37:3

Esther, who wasn't afraid of the truth,

> Queen Esther replied, "If I have found favor with the king, and if it pleases the king to grant my request, I ask that my life and the lives of my people will be spared." Esther 7:3

and David's great-grandma, a woman named Ruth.

> He [Obed, the son of Ruth and Boaz] became the father of Jesse and the grandfather of David. Ruth 4:17

That isn't all that the Bible can hold.
It's where all the stories of Jesus are told.

> This is the Good News about Jesus the Messiah, the Son of God. Mark 1:1

> This disciple is the one who testifies to these events and has recorded them here. And we know that his account of these things is accurate. Jesus also did many other things. If they were all written down, I suppose the whole world could not contain the books that would be written. John 21:24-25

Learn of his birth on the first Christmas Day.

> While they were there, the time came for her baby to be born. She gave birth to her first child, a son. Luke 2:6-7

Meet a few friends that he made on his way.

One day as Jesus was walking along the shore of the Sea of Galilee, he saw two brothers—Simon, also called Peter, and Andrew—throwing a net into the water, for they fished for a living. Matthew 4:18

As Jesus and the disciples continued on their way to Jerusalem, they came to a certain village where a woman named Martha welcomed him into her home. Her sister, Mary, sat at the Lord's feet, listening to what he taught. Luke 10:38-39

When Jesus came by, he looked up at Zacchaeus and called him by name. "Zacchaeus!" he said. "Quick, come down! I must be a guest in your home today." Zacchaeus quickly climbed down and took Jesus to his house in great excitement and joy. Luke 19:5-6

He walked on the water and calmed down the sea,

When Jesus woke up, he rebuked the wind and the raging waves. Suddenly the storm stopped and all was calm. Luke 8:24

About three o'clock in the morning Jesus came toward [the disciples], walking on the water. . . . He climbed into the boat, and the wind stopped. They were totally amazed. Mark 6:48, 51

talked to the children who sat by his knee.

> Jesus called a little child to him and put the child among them. Matthew 18:2

> One day some parents brought their children to Jesus so he could lay his hands on them and pray for them. . . . Jesus said, "Let the children come to me. Don't stop them! For the Kingdom of Heaven belongs to those who are like these children." Matthew 19:13-14

Then comes the story that God loves the best.
It's really no secret—perhaps you have guessed!
It's the story of how Jesus died on the cross.

> For God loved the world so much that he gave his one and only Son. John 3:16

> It was written long ago that the Messiah would suffer and die and rise from the dead on the third day. Luke 24:46

It starts as a story of sadness and loss.

> Mary was standing outside the tomb crying. John 20:11

But early on Easter, folks saw with their eyes
that Jesus had risen—oh, what a surprise!

> Then the angel spoke to the women. "Don't be afraid!" he said. "I know you are looking for Jesus, who was crucified. He isn't here! He is risen from the dead, just as he said would happen." Matthew 28:5-6

Why are you looking among the dead for someone who is alive? He isn't here! He is risen from the dead! Luke 24:5-6

God gave new life to our Savior, his Son.
What an incredible thing God has done!

Give thanks to the LORD, for he is good! His faithful love endures forever. Psalm 136:1

[Christ] was raised from the dead on the third day, just as the Scriptures said. 1 Corinthians 15:4

You may see Bibles in pink, blue, or green.
Some are so fancy, they're fit for a queen!
It doesn't matter what color you choose.
Inside, you'll find God's amazing Good News.

The Good News about the Kingdom will be preached throughout the whole world, so that all nations will hear it. Matthew 24:14

God promised this Good News long ago through his prophets in the holy Scriptures. Romans 1:2

The love that God has for us shines through and through.
And that's how we know that the Bible is true!

The light shines in the darkness, and the darkness can never extinguish it. John 1:5

Every word of God proves true. Proverbs 30:5

See how very much our Father loves us, for he calls us his children, and that is what we are! 1 John 3:1

Some people read it all, line after line.
Others may skip around—both ways are fine.
What matters more is to read it and then
to go back and read it again and again!

My child, pay attention to what I say. Listen carefully to my words. Don't lose sight of them. Let them penetrate deep into your heart. Proverbs 4:20-21

You don't need puzzles and games when you read.
Learning the stories is all that you need.

They delight in the law of the LORD, meditating on it day and night. Psalm 1:2

God does not ask you to know it all now.
Just try to live as the Bible shows how.

Your word is a lamp to guide my feet and a light for my path. Psalm 119:105

If your Bible wears out, it is really all right—
God thinks it's great when you read it each night!
No other book will replace it, no, never.
The Bible—God's Word—will be with us forever!

The grass withers and the flowers fade, but the word of our God stands forever. Isaiah 40:8

Heaven and earth will disappear, but my words will never disappear. Matthew 24:35; Mark 13:31; Luke 21:33

About the Author

Kathleen Bostrom has been an ordained minister in the Presbyterian Church (USA) since 1983. She and her husband, Greg, have served as copastors of Wildwood Presbyterian Church in Wildwood, Illinois, since 1991.

Kathy has won awards for preaching and is often requested to speak to groups at the national level. She has published numerous articles in various journals and newspapers, and is the author of over a dozen books for children. *Who Is Jesus?* was a finalist for the 2000 Gold Medallion Award, and *What about Heaven?* was nominated for the People's Choice Award. Kathy's books have sold well over one million copies.

Kathy has been a board member of the Presbyterian Writers Guild since 1998 and has served as president. She is also a member of the Society of Children's Book Writers and Illustrators.

Kathy earned a master of arts in Christian education and a master of divinity from Princeton Theological Seminary, and a doctor of ministry in preaching from McCormick Theological Seminary in Chicago.

Kathy and Greg have three children: Christopher, Amy, and David.

About the Illustrator

Elena Kucharik, well-known Care Bears artist, has created the Little Blessings characters that appear in the line of Little Blessings products for young children and their families.

Born in Cleveland, Ohio, Elena received a bachelor of fine arts degree in commercial art at Kent State University. After graduation she worked as a greeting card artist and art director at American Greetings Corporation in Cleveland.

For most of her career, Elena has been a freelance illustrator. She was the lead artist and developer of Care Bears, as well as a designer and illustrator for major corporations and publishers. Most recently Elena has been focusing her talents on illustrations for children's books.

Elena and her husband live in Madison, Connecticut. They have two grown daughters and three adorable grandchildren.

Books in the Little Blessings line

- *Prayers for Little Hearts*
- *Questions from Little Hearts*

- *What Is God Like?*
- *Who Is Jesus?*
- *What about Heaven?*
- *Are Angels Real?*
- *What Is Prayer?*
- *Is God Always with Me?*
- *Why Is There a Cross?*
- *What Is the Bible?*
- *Who Made the World?*

- *The One Year Devotions for Preschoolers*
- *The One Year Devotions for Preschoolers 2*
  (available soon)

- *God Loves You*
- *Thank You, God!*
- *Many-Colored Blessings*
- *Blessings Come in Shapes*

- *God Created Me!*
  A memory book of baby's first year

CP0216